This book belongs to:

_____

FAMILY TREE

The Greatest Gift is Family

PARENT NAME

PARENT NAME

SIBLINGS

GRANDPARENTS  GRANDPARENTS

AUNTS & UNCLES

AUNTS & UNCLES

YOUR STORY
Our Journey to You

How We Found You:

Our Journey To Meet You:

What You Mean To Us:

YOUR FOREVER FAMILY

Love you for always...

MOMMY

DADDY

BABY

All About Mommy

FULL NAME   BIRTHDAY

WHERE I GREW UP

MY FAVORITE CHILDHOOD MEMORIES

MY INTERESTS & HOBBIES

WHAT I WANT YOU TO KNOW ABOUT ME

Love Letter From Mommy

NEVER FORGET...

I'LL LOVE YOU forever I'LL LIKE YOU FOR always AS LONG AS I'M LIVING MY Baby YOU'LL BE.

MY DREAM FOR YOU...

All About Daddy

FULL NAME   BIRTHDAY

WHERE I GREW UP

MY FAVORITE CHILDHOOD MEMORIES

MY INTERESTS & HOBBIES

WHAT I WANT YOU TO KNOW ABOUT ME

Love Letter From Daddy

_____
_____
_____
_____
_____
_____
_____
_____

NEVER FORGET...

Love Story

MY DREAM FOR YOU...

MEMORIES OF YOU
Your First Year Photo Checklist

FIRST YEAR PHOTO CHECKLIST:

Our first day with you	Baby in nursery
Baby's first bath	First feeding
First family photo	Baby's first outfit
Baby's hands with ours	Baby & Daddy
Baby & Mommy	Baby with Grandparents
Baby's first doctor visit	Baby with siblings
Baby's first haircut	Baby sitting up
Learning to crawl	Baby sleeping
Baby's first time standing	Baby's first birthday party
Baby giving kisses	Getting into mischief!
Baby with favorite toy	Baby in the car seat

OTHER PHOTO IDEAS:

MILESTONES
Watching You Grow

Lifts Head:

Age:

Smiles:

Age:

Rolls onto Back:

Age:

Laughs:

Age:

Grasps Objects:

Age:

Says Mama:

Age:

Sleeps Through the Night:

Age:

Reaches for Objects:

Age:

Discovers Hands & Feet:

Age:

Coos & Babbles:

Age:

First Tooth:

Age:

Eats Solid Food:

Age:

Says Dada:

Age:

Pulls up to standing position:

Age:

MILESTONES
Watching You Grow

Takes a few steps:

Age:

First word with understanding:

Age:

Turns towards sounds:

Age:

Points to named things:

Age:

Recognizes Family Members

Age:

Kicks a ball:

Age:

Shakes head for yes or no:

Age:

Takes first step unassisted:

Age:

Sits without support:

Age:

Likes to look into mirror:

Age:

Builds block towers:

Age:

Drinks from a cup:

Age:

Watching you grow is our greatest joy...

	Height:	Weight:
1 MONTH		
2 MONTHS		
3 MONTHS		
4 MONTHS		
5 MONTHS		

Watching you grow is our greatest joy...

Height: ### Weight:

6 MONTHS

7 MONTHS

8 MONTHS

9 MONTHS

10 MONTHS

Watching you grow is our greatest joy...

	Height:	Weight:
11 MONTHS		
12 MONTHS		
13 MONTHS		
14 MONTHS		
15 MONTHS		

Watching you grow is our greatest joy...

	Height:	Weight:
16 MONTHS		
17 MONTHS		
18 MONTHS		
19 MONTHS		
20 MONTHS		

	Height:	Weight:
21 MONTHS		
22 MONTHS		
23 MONTHS		
24 MONTHS		

Two years of beautiful memories

REFLECTIONS:

You're our greatest gift...

MONTH 1	THOUGHTS

MONTH 2	THOUGHTS

MONTH 3	THOUGHTS

MONTH 4	THOUGHTS

MONTH 5	THOUGHTS

You're our pride & joy...

MONTH 6	THOUGHTS

MONTH 7	THOUGHTS

MONTH 8	THOUGHTS

MONTH 9	THOUGHTS

MONTH 10	THOUGHTS

You're our everything...

MONTH 11

THOUGHTS

MONTH 12

THOUGHTS

Our Favorite Memories

Photos to Remember

1 ^{Year} Old ♡

2 ^{Years} Old ♡

Photos to Remember

3 *Years Old* ♡

4 *Years Old* ♡

YOUR FIRST YEAR
Love You to the Moon & Back

ALL ABOUT YOU

WEIGHT:

HEIGHT:

FAV FOOD:

FAV ACTIVITY:

THE WORLD YOU LIVE IN

TOP SONGS:

HEADLINES:

WORLD LEADERS:

YEARLY MILESTONES

YOUR FAVORITE THINGS

WHAT WE DID TO CELEBRATE

YEAR ONE PHOTO
Your Smile Fills Our Hearts

Love
is
forever

YEAR IN REVIEW
We Never Want to Miss a Thing

SLEEPS SOUNDLY

LIFTS HEAD

PLAYS WITH TOYS

LIFTS UPPER BODY

ROLLS OVER

BEGINS TO TALK

BEGINS TO CRAWL

SITTING UP

YEAR ONE THOUGHTS & FEELINGS

YEAR TWO PHOTO
A Love that Lasts Forever

ALL YOU
need
IS
love

YEAR THREE PHOTO

You're the light of our lives

YEAR FOUR PHOTO

Twinkle twinkle, little star...

YEAR FIVE PHOTO
Mommy's Angel, Daddy's Joy

Photos to Remember

1 $^{Year}_{Old}$ ♡

2 $^{Years}_{Old}$ ♡

Photos to Remember

3 *Year's Old* ♡

4 *Year's Old* ♡

Made in United States
North Haven, CT
27 October 2022

25948728R00083